Let There Be Light

Unreal Engine 4 Tutorial Book

by

Sergei

Lezhnevich

About The Book

The better way to learn something is a practice.

You probably heard from some people a phrase - read documentation, everything is written in that. Well actually this is partially good enough advice.
But you know what?
I read only parts of it. Because I always wanted to do the things that never written anywhere. Very often the things that I wanted to do never written in any documentation.

In this book, I will learn you how to work with Unreal Engine **Light Actors**
You will learn how to create:

- **Rechargeable Flashlight**
- **Interactable Light Switcher**
- **Trace for Objects in optimized way**
- **Parent Actors and Child Actors**
- **Destroyable Light Actors via Custom Events**
- **Destroying light via shooting**

I want to help you to go throw the path of learning. I also learning with you. I write such a book for the first time, but no matter what I will guide you, it is a long way to get learn, fixing mistakes and bugs… and finding the best solutions and I really want you to succeed, as you succeed, me either!

So don't get stuck! Let me guide you and help you to make the Cool things!

About The Author

My name is **Sergei Lezhnevich**
I am self-taught developer.
Despite that fact, I am currently **leading programmist-designer** in the **Xtrematic** company, I can make any impossible task.

Working in the game industry more than **6 years.**
I believe, that even if you don't have a specific knowledge about Game making, but you have a desire to learn, than **I can teach to do it!**

Follow the Light!

Let me say some really **basics** about the Light in Unreal Engine 4
I won't go in the theory very deep or talking about graphics or design.
Just really cool things that will help you to plan **the optimization** of your game working with light actors.

There are **3 types** of Light Actors:
Static Light
Stationary Light
Movable Light
Each Light has some impact on performance an the way how it can be used.
Static Light
The primary use case for static lights is for low power devices on mobile platforms.
Stationary Lights
are lights that are intended to stay in one position, but are able to change in other ways, such as their brightness and color. This is the primary way in which they differ from **Static Lights**, which cannot change in any way during gameplay. **Stationary Lights** tend to

have the highest quality, medium mutability, and medium performance cost. **Movable Lights** cast completely dynamic light and shadows, can change position, rotation, color, brightness, falloff, radius, and just about every other property they have.

Keep it in mind when you work with Light. If you Want to be able to make any Manipulations with Light via Blueprints You should use **Stationary Lights** less **Movable Lights** as they have the highest performance cost

In the beginning

Each game has an environment, has some rocks, walls, grass, characters and ect.
We see how it shapes, textures, geometry how it looks, acts and the good thing that allows us to see such beauty or horror is the light.
As I said I won't touch any graphic technics, style or design rules.
You probably have your own vision.
Our purpose is to **learn how to code** and how to control such a powerful power - THE LIGHT
The skills that we will receive from this book course will allow us to control the light in many ways as we want, creating great variety of it usage and bunch ways to create an atmosphere, to catch player's attention, create an effect of life in the world, give to player the ability to effect on the environment, to get the connection between fiction world and player.

FlashLight

Let's say, you would love to create a horror game, you probably intent to make it scary and dark and mysterious. Constant lack of light and something scary crawling in the dark, make player get curious, to see what is going on there in the dark or run away from it. Let's give him a Flashlight!

FlashLight: SETUP

For this tutorial I will use the **18 version of Unreal Engine**
I am sure there is already even fresher version of it, but still what we will do, will work on any versions of Engines.

I create a pure new project with **First person shooter template.**
You may work with your own project, it really does not matter.

For convenience, I will create:

- **A separate folder** and call it TUTORIAL
- Create a **Map** and call it ROOM
- In the World settings Set the Standard First Person Game Mode (To Open World Settings go to Windows -> World Settings)
- Create a simple **Floor** from a cube via scale

- Place a **Player Start**

And as a final part just add **3 point lights**

Green - **Static Light**

Yellow - **Stationary Light**

Red - **Movable Light**

As Clear reminder for us, With what Light we will work

In The Content folder, Find a standard Character **FirstPersonCharacter**, you may use Blueprint filter.

Go to ViewPort

The Character already has some components, As I work in frames of tutorial, I Will work with standard template without any serious changes.

You should take it into consideration. If you have your own components, you may work with them, but keep in mind the names of variables that we will use.

I have a skeletal mesh **component** called **FP_Gun.**

Let's

- Add a **light component** to our character (a **SpotLight**)
- Attach The **SpotLight** it to our **FP_Gun** gun
- Adjust Location and Rotation of **SpotLight** properly
- Set **SpotLight** as **Movable Light**

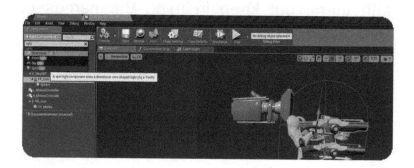

We will get the following result:

We can walk around with a light that comes from our weapon

As simple as it is! The Basic FlashLight is Done!

FlashLight: CODE

Now let's make some code! A possibility to **turn ON/OFF** our Flashlight

Go to **Event Graph**
Make a function that will be called by pressing **F key**
- **F key** Pressed Make a logic - If our Light is turned ON than turn it OFF and **vice versa**

The main point is **not to use** a **flip/flop** node because if you make **Save/Load game**, it may work not in a proper way. Instead of this we will use a **check** with written values in advance.

Make a FlashLight intensity by **default 0**

Thus Our Logic Will looks like this
- Get **SpotLight** intensity
- Check if intensity is equal to 0 -> Set **SpotLight** intensity to specific Value if not equal (Thus it means the **SpotLight**

is turned ON) -> Set **SpotLight** intensity to 0

At the End of Our Logic Chain, we will additionally add **play sound 2D**
You may use any sounds as you wish.

The scheme is looked like this
There are no branches nodes as you might get used. instead of them I use **Select Node**
This helps a lot to make the chains it more clear and remove the necessity to create bunches of variables that need to be set.

Now you have a possibility to create a **FlashLight**,
You may tweak it as you want, in any suitable way for you.

In our case we will add **a battery** to our **FlashLight**

Let's make The Light of our FlashLight getting weaker or stronger if it don't have enough of battery
and
Recharge the battery in two ways:
Slowly - with some period of time the battery is getting it power back
Faster - simple reload by pressing button, like we set a new battery

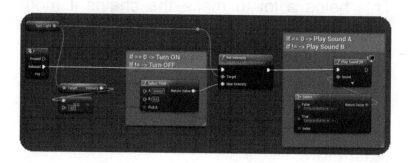

Don't get lost, it easier than it might be seen.
Faster Way
- Create a **float** variable of Our Light Power and call it **LightPower**
- Set it to your any value I set 5000 as default and
- Plug **LightPower** value to **A** float

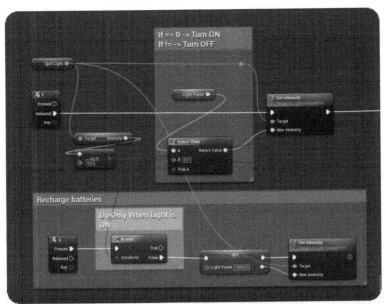

- Create a **Q Key** (We will use it to reload the power of our battery)
- On **Q Key** pressed with a check to work only when the FlashLight is turned ON **Set Light Power Intensity** To initial Highest value
- Apply Value of **LightPower** to our **SpotLight**

The Scheme Turn On/Off of FlashLight

Slower   **Way**

We will create **a timer** that will reduce the power of light and bring it back.

We will create **two states** that affects our Light Intensity:
1-st one - minus intensity
2-nd one - plus intensity

This time we will use **the gates** and **delay**
  - Make a check If our **SpotLight** Intensity **is 0** then make **Recharge** the power of battery
  - If our Check says that our **SpotLight** intensity **is greater than 0** (in fact the light is on) than **Reduce** the power of battery

The Logic itself goes increase and decrease the **LightPower Value** with a certain delay.
Depending on the check we launch Branch A or B
  - Use a sequence node
  - Then 0 - Open the gate (Launch that we need)
  - Then 1 - Close the gate (Close the second gate)
  - Then 2 - Enter the Gate (Allow the logic to execute)
The logic in Each Gate is set up in a loop.

It executes itself continuously until the intensity will reach the certain value.

The Gate A - increase the **LightPower** until the 5000 value. There are no set of **SpotLight** intensity as soon as it works only when the light is switched off.

The Gate B - decrease the **LightPower** until the 0 value and set **SpotLight** intensity to new

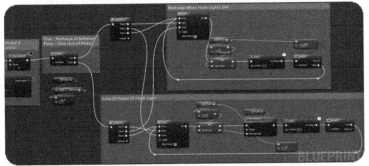

decreased value each time.

As soon as **Gate A** is opened, the sequence node Close the **Gate B**, preventing the **Gate B** logic and vice versa, so there are no any conflict.

The **delay** value - 0.1
and
The **increase/decrease** value - 30
You may set any other values as you wish

Thus the scheme of Rechargeable FlashLight

Light Switcher

We take an example - **a horror game**.

The player enters into the room, darkness surrounds him, the moonlight is a hope that helps to see the path, but it is not enough. The Player desperately needs to find a switcher to turn on the light, to see the path!
Or maybe not!
The player entered into the room... The Player is hiding from someone...
It is better to turn off the light, to try to sneak from the chaser…
NEED TO FIND A SWITCHER

Trace

Let's have a look from the point of view of our character.
To make any interactions with any objects in the world, we need to perceive them.

Make Character Look at something and decide to interact with it or no and how if yes.

Basically we will create a **trace of dynamic objects**.

As Our **dynamic objects** objects it will be **Blueprint actors**.

Go to our **FirstPersonCharacter** Blueprint

- On **Tick Event** Create **LineTraceForObjects**
- Set Trace **Object Type** as **WorldDynamic**
- As for the **Start Point** of Trace, it will the **Sphere** component
- As for the **End Point** of Trace, it will be the sum of the following components: **FirstPesronCamera** Rotation it's Forward Vector multiplied by float as the distance to 500 units. The **Result** of it plus the **Start Point** equals **End Point**

- On Trace Execute make a **check** If it **HIT** something or **NOT**
- Create a variable of type **Actor** and name it as you want for example **HitActor**

Thus If there is something we hit we overwrite the **HitActor** variable, making it empty or not. (Make our trace **Visible** as For One Frame **for debugging**)

The Scheme of Trace

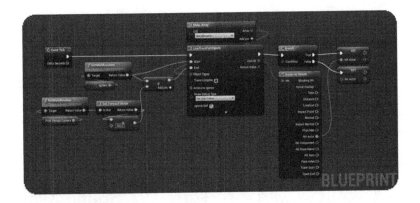

Next we create a **Blueprint Actor** and call it **Switcher_Master**

This will be our parent Blueprint actor with main functions. When we will create child blueprint actors, they will **share** the same functions and variables from it's parent **Blueprint Actor.** This will give us more mobility and optimisation. As we don't need to do cast each time to different Blueprint Actors.

In the Main Blueprint Actor **Switcher_Master**
Next
Create:

- **Float** variable **Light Intensity** (set it default value any you wish)
- **Audio** variable **Turn On Sound** (set any audio file as you want)
- **Audio** variable **Turn Off Sound** (set any audio file as you want)

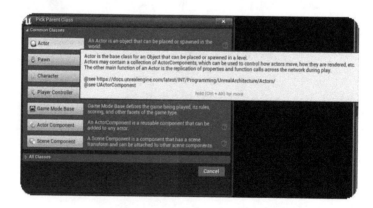

- **Light** Actor (Will be picked from the map)
- Make all these variables as **public**

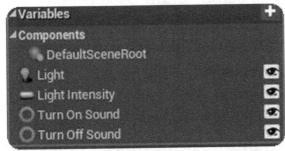

These variables will help us create **Dynamic Child Actors**, that uses different Point Light Actors in the world, with different intensity and in case different turn ON/OFF sounds

Function

Create a function that switches the light intensity of selected **Light** Actor from the World. The main body of the function will be almost the same as we did with **Flash Light.**
We get The Specific Light Actor, check it intensity and set intensity and play the sound. But you need to remember that only **Stationary Lights** and **Movable Lights** can be changed via blueprint.

- Create a function and called it **Switch The Light**
- Get **Light** Actor, Get it intensity (If the Intensity equals to 0 we Set It Intensity to **Float Light Intensity** variable. If the Intensity is greater than 0, then set Light Intensity to 0)
- At the End of the logic add node **Play Sound 2D**

The Final Look Of the function With created Variables

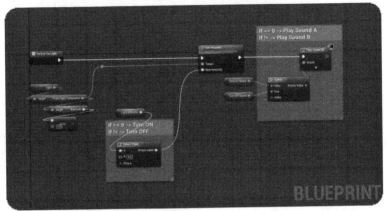

27

Now let's create a Switcher itself.

- Create a **Child Actor** from our **Switcher_Master** and called it

Wall_Switcher
- Add a **Static Mesh** component (a cube would be enough, this will be roughly a representative of wall switcher)
- Place **Wall_Switcher** to the map
- Place **Point Light Actor** to the map and Pick it or any an existing **Point Light Actor** On the Map (The blueprint function created earlier **Switch The Light** will affect to picked **Point Light Actor**)

Wall_Switcher

Interaction

Now we already have a line trace of **Dynamic Objects** thus we can interact with Wall_Swithcher, because it has a **static mesh** with **collision** type of Dynamic Object by default.

Our interaction will be via **E key**
  - On **E key** Pressed Do a check - If our trace actor called **Hit Actor** is valid? (basically is it empty or not)
  - If Valid than we get the class of the actor and check does **Hit Actor** belongs to our **Switcher_Master**. If true we do a cast to **Switcher_Master** and call a general function **Switch The Light**

We could just cast to **Switcher Master** from the trace, but the main point of that check is the **Mobility** and Code **Optimisation**.
This will help to add additional checks in case we have many Different Actors to interact With.

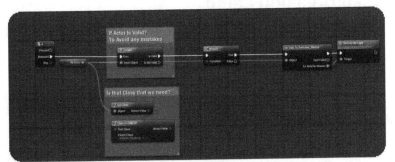

Like **Chests** or **NPC**

The Scheme of E Key Interaction

Breaking Light

Now as We Understand the main point of Usage of the function **Switch The Light** and **Child Actors** we can move further in more creative way

Like Breaking Lamp.

Imagine, you enter into the room, sudden there is power surge and the light brakes.

Or

You enter into the room and The Light sudden become turned ON and you a NPC who stands near the switcher with ready for you a quest.

The other **usages**

will be depend on your designer point of view and task

For Example like...

- distract the player or the enemy
- take off the possibility to clear see the opponent
- and many other things

Our case, take off the **possibility to clear see** plus

Flickering effect, like our lamp has a power surge, there is something wrong with Electricity, perhaps a Ghost!

Before

- Create **Flickering Material** and call it **Light_Flicker**
- Select the appeared bunch of nodes and in the **Details Panel** Set Material Domain as **Light Function**

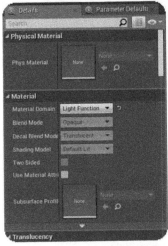

- And in the Main **Graph Body**
- Call **Time,** Multiply it by 1, **sine** it (value 0.5), **Frac** it and you get result of Flickering Light

Sounds scary but it quite simple, here is **the scheme**

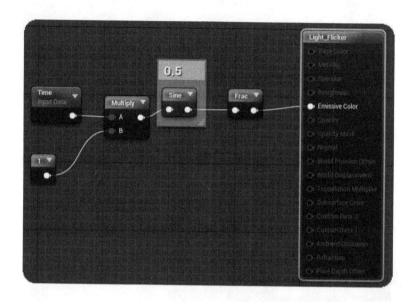

Thus, Moving on to our blueprint:

- Create a child blueprint from our Parent Blueprint Actor **Swithcer_Master** and call it **Overlap_Switcher**
- add an **Overlap box component** with default name **Box**

The principle of this blueprint is almost the same.

- Place it on the level
- Pick The **Point Light Actor**
- Our **Box** component on **Begin Overlap** Launch The Function **Switch The Light**

As we enter into our **Trigger Box**,

- Make a check. Is an **Actor** entered into **Trigger Box** is a Player? (This need to prevent to be interacted by any other blueprint actor)
- Make even Once via **Do Once** node (This will launch the logic once, but if we need somehow call it again we make a **check**)
- Get **Light** Actor variable get it **Point Light Component**
- Set **Light Function Material** Set What we created earlier
- With a Small **Delay** Clear **Light Function Material** by setting it Null (Thus make our Light Flicker Like something is wrong with electricity and then turn it Off)
- Call the Function **Switch The Light**
- Create a **bool** variable and call it **Repeatable?** (Can Event ever launched again?)
- If True, with delay in 5 seconds Set **Light** Actor, it's **Point Light Component** Intensity back to your float value **Light Intensity**

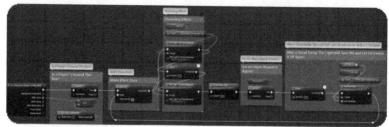

- Then **Plug** the end of the logic to the beginning of **Do Once** into **Reset** case

The Overlapping Switch The Light With Light Flickering

Shoot The Light

We have a gun isn't it?
How we would like.. use it? Why not brake some lamps?

- Create Child Blueprint **Actor** from our **Switch_Master** Parent Blueprint, called it **Lamp**
- **Lamp** blueprint will have the function **Switch The Light**, but we won't use it, we create a pure new one
- Create a function and call it **Destroy Lamp**
- You may Use **Point Light Actors** From The Map or Add **Point Light Component** to This Blueprint
- Add any **Static Mesh** component In our Case **Cube** would be enough
- In the **Destroy Lamp** Function Get **Your Point Light Actor** or **Point Light Component** and Set it intensity to 0.
- Than Add node **Play Sound at Location.** As the Location put **Get World Location** of **Cube**

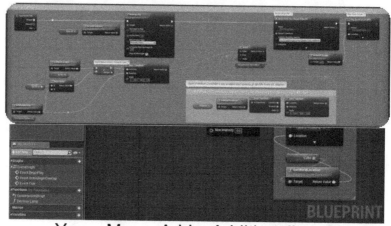

- You May Add Additionally **Spawn Emitter At Location** Like Particle of sparks or something else

Next is to call this function. We will do it when shooting
There are generally two ways to shoot
1 - **Via Projectile**
2 - **Via Trace**
For simplicity I will use the 1-st method
The Details of shooting are out of bounds of this Book

Our weapon already has some logic to shoot

We will leave it as it is.

We need only to work with spawnable actor called **FirstPersonProjectile**
This blueprint physically can move in our 3D dimension, we will use it but add a check when it collides with something in the world

- Go to **FirstPersonProjectile** blueprint
- Create a **Tick Event**
- On Tick Event call node **Sphere Trace By Channel** Set The **Visibility** Channel
- Set The **Start** and **End** location values from **Actor Location**
- Set The **Radius** Float
- Make a **Check** if It Hit Something Or Not
- If True Check What Actor it hits.
- **Get** Its **Class,** Is this Class is Child of **Lamp**
- If True, make a **Cast to Lamp Blueprint Actor** and call the function **Destroy Lamp** Blueprint Actor Is It Blueprint Actor from
- For testing purposes make our trace **visible for one frame**

The Scheme of Tracing of Channel

Now, place the **Lamps** to the level.
It time to shoot!

Conclusion

That is it. Hope You Enjoyed This Tutorial Series Book. Got Some new Info and learned new things about Blueprint Actors, the ways to optimize and organize your code.

If that so, please let me know, leave a comment or something like that.

With all that stuff you have learned you may create a huge bunch of gameplay in your game.

Hope you to see you in my next tutorial book series.

My Social Media Contacts

#Lezhnevich

FaceBook:
https://www.facebook.com/Lezhnevich.Sergei
E-mail: sergei.lezhnevich@gmail.com
YouTubeChannel:
https://www.youtube.com/c/SergeiLezhnevich